Bears Have Cubs

by Elizabeth Dana Jaffe

Animals and Their Young

Content Adviser: Janann Jenner, Ph.D.

Science Adviser: Terrence E. Young Jr., M.Ed., M.L.S.,
Jefferson Parish (La.) Public Schools

Reading Adviser: Dr. Linda D. Labbo,
Department of Reading Education,
College of Education, The University of Georgia

COMPASS POINT BOOKS

Minneapolis, Minnesota

Compass Point Books
3722 West 50th Street, #115
Minneapolis, MN 55410

Visit Compass Point Books on the Internet at *www.compasspointbooks.com* or e-mail your request to
custserv@compasspointbooks.com

Photographs ©: Richard Day/Daybreak Imagery, cover; Robert McCaw, 4, 12, 14; Stephen J. Lang/Visuals Unlimited, 6; Raymond Gehman/Corbis, 8; Bob Schillereff, 10; Kennan Ward/Corbis, 16; Gerard Fuehrer/Visuals Unlimited, 18; Cheryl A. Ertelt, 20.

Editors: E. Russell Primm, Emily J. Dolbear, and Laura Driscoll
Photo Researchers: Svetlana Zhurkina and Jo Miller
Photo Selector: Linda S. Koutris
Designer: Bradfordesign, Inc.

Library of Congress Cataloging-in-Publication Data

Jaffe, Elizabeth Dana.
    Bears have cubs / by Elizabeth D. Jaffe.
        p. cm. — (Animals and their young)
    Includes bibliographical references (p.).
    Summary: Describes the birth, growth, development, and reproduction of bears.
    ISBN 0-7565-0168-7 (hardcover)
        1. Bears—Infancy—Juvenile literature. [1. Bears. 2. Animals—Infancy.] I. Title. II. Series.
QL737.C27 J34 2002
599.78—dc21
                                                          2001004131

Table of Contents

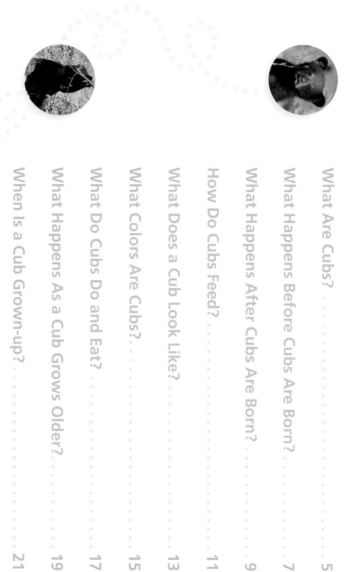

Cubs are baby bears. A bear is a large, strong animal with thick fur.

There are seven kinds of bears. This book is about the American black bear. It is a common type of bear in North America.

Bears are shy animals. They try to stay away from people. In the wild, most bears live alone. Mother bears live with their cubs.

A black bear

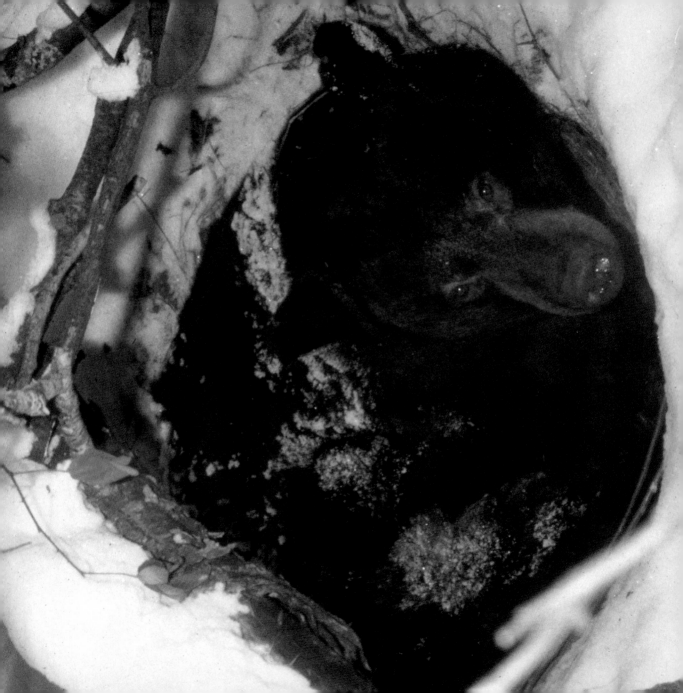

What Happens Before Cubs Are Born?

In the fall, all bears get ready for winter. They eat a lot. Their bodies get fat.

Then each bear finds a dry and cozy **den**. This may be a cave or a hole in the ground. The bear spends the winter sleeping in the den. It does not eat or drink all winter.

Unborn cubs grow inside their mother's body. She carries them for about seven months.

An adult bear during its winter sleep

What Happens After Cubs Are Born?

The mother bear wakes up in her den during January or February. She gives birth to her cubs. A mother bear may have one to four cubs at a time.

Cubs have very little fur at birth. Their eyes are also closed. Each cub weighs less than 1 pound (0.5 kilogram). They are tiny and helpless.

The cubs stay in the den with their mother for two to three months. They cuddle up close to their mother to keep warm.

An American black bear cub in its den

How Do Cubs Feed?

Newborn bears drink milk from their mother's body. This is called **nursing**. The mother bear's milk is rich and creamy. It helps the cubs grow and get stronger.

Sometimes the mother bear sleeps as her cubs nurse. She is careful when she moves around. She makes sure to keep her weight off of her cubs.

A mother bear with her nursing cubs

What Does a Cub Look Like?

At two months old, a bear cub weighs between 4 and 10 pounds (2 and 4.5 kilograms). Now it looks like its parents, only smaller.

A young cub is covered in thick fur. It has small, black eyes. It has small ears and a short tail. A cub's **snout** is shorter than an adult bear's snout.

Cubs have four paws. Each paw has five toes. Each toe has a sharp, curved claw.

This bear cub looks like a small grown-up bear.

What Colors Are Cubs?

American black bears are not always black. Most cubs have black, dark brown, or red-brown fur. A few may have pale blue or white fur! These bears usually live in snowy areas.

Many cubs have brown fur around their snouts. Some have a patch of white fur on their chests.

American black bears from the same family can be different colors.

What Do Cubs Do and Eat?

Cubs come out of the den when they are two or three months old. They love to play with one another. They learn from their mother how to catch fish to eat. They stay close to her. She is always looking out for danger.

Cubs like to taste what their mother eats. They live on mother's milk until they are about six months old. Then they start to eat some solid food.

Older bears eat almost anything. They enjoy meat, fruit, insects—and honey!

A black bear catches a fish to eat.

A bear cub grows very quickly in the first few months. Its snout gets longer. Its fur gets thicker.

After eight months, a cub stops nursing. Then it eats only solid food. A nine-month-old cub weighs up to 165 pounds (75 kilograms).

Most cubs stay with their mother until they are between eighteen and twenty-four months old. Then the mother bear is ready to have new cubs. She chases the older cubs away. Now they are on their own.

This bear is eating crab apples from a branch.

When Is a Cub Grown-up?

A bear reaches its full size when it is about three years old. Most female bears begin having cubs when they are three or four years old.

Most adult bears are 4 to 7 feet (1.2 to 2.1 meters) tall when they stand on their back legs. They weigh from 90 to 660 pounds (41 to 300 kilograms). Bears in zoos grow even bigger! An American black bear can live to be more than thirty years old.

Glossary

cubs—baby bears

den—a bear's winter home, usually a cave or an underground hole

nursing—drinking milk produced by the mother

snout—the long front part of an animal's head, which includes its nose, mouth, and jaw

Did You Know?

- When black bears are scared, they usually climb trees.

- A tired bear cub may crawl on its mother's back to be carried.

- Black bears are good swimmers.

- Bear cubs sometimes make a purring sound while they nurse.

Want to Know More?

At the Library

Betz, Dieter. *The Bear Family*. New York: Tambourine Books, 1991.

Patent, Dorothy Hinshaw. *Looking at Bears*. New York: Holiday House, 1994.

Pope, Joyce. *Nature Club: Animal Babies*. Mahwah, N.J.: Troll Associates, 1994.

Wallace, Karen. *Wild Baby Animals*. New York: Dorling Kindersley, 2000.

On the Web

Language and Sounds of Black Bears

http://www.bear.org/Kids/Sounds.html

For audio files of the many sounds that American black bears make

Alaska Department of Fish and Game: Bear Facts

http://www.state.ak.us/adfg/wildlife/geninfo/game/bearfax.htm

For tips on what to do if you meet a bear in the wild

Through the Mail

North American Bear Society

P.O. Box 55774

Phoenix, AZ 85078

To get more information about the different kinds of bears that live in North America

On the Road

Vince Shute Wildlife Sanctuary

P.O. Box 77

Orr, MN 55771

218/757-0172

To see American black bears in their natural habitat

Index

About the Author
After graduating from Brown University, Elizabeth Dana Jaffe received her master's degree in early education from Bank Street College of Education. Since then, she has written and edited educational materials. Elizabeth Dana Jaffe lives in New York City.